WHEN DID
IGNORANCE
BECOME A POINT OF VIEW?

Other DILBERT books from Andrews McMeel Publishing

Excuse Me While I Wag
ISBN: 0-7407-1390-6

Dilbert-A Treasury of Sunday Strips: Version 00
ISBN: 0-7407-0531-8

Random Acts of Management
ISBN: 0-7407-0453-2

Dilbert Gives You the Business
ISBN: 0-7407-0338-2 hardcover
ISBN: 0-7407-0003-0 paperback

Don't Step in the Leadership
ISBN: 0-8362-7844-5

Journey to Cubeville
ISBN: 0-8362-7175-0 hardcover
ISBN: 0-8362-6745-1 paperback

I'm Not Anti-Business, I'm Anti-Idiot
ISBN: 0-8362-5182-2

Seven Years of Highly Defective People
ISBN: 0-8362-5129-6 hardcover
ISBN: 0-8362-3668-8 paperback

Casual Day Has Gone Too Far
ISBN: 0-8362-2899-5

Fugitive from the Cubicle Police
ISBN: 0-8362-2119-2

Still Pumped from Using the Mouse
ISBN: 0-8362-1026-3

It's Obvious You Won't Survive by Your Wits Alone
ISBN: 0-8362-0415-8

Bring Me the Head of Willy the Mailboy!
ISBN: 0-8362-1779-9

Shave the Whales
ISBN: 0-8362-1740-3

Dogbert's Clues for the Clueless
ISBN: 0-8362-1737-3

Build a Better Life by Stealing Office Supplies
ISBN: 0-8362-1757-8

Always Postpone Meetings with Time-Wasting Morons
ISBN: 0-8362-1758-6

For ordering information, call 1-800-642-6480.

WHEN DID IGNORANCE BECOME A POINT OF VIEW?

A DILBERT™ BOOK
BY SCOTT ADAMS

Andrews McMeel
Publishing

Kansas City

For Tom-a-to and Tom-ah-to's mother

Introduction

Recently a woman called me and said she had no idea who I was but she had been told by someone—she couldn't remember who—that I give money to people like her. The woman said that she and her husband had nine kids and had moved to a desert in the Middle East. Now they were having difficulty supporting themselves because, well, they had nine kids and had moved to a desert. She figured the best solution was to call me and ask if I would support the entire family indefinitely. If you have nine children and think it's a good idea to move to the desert it is fair to say that you are not a good decision maker. So the question I had to ask myself was this: If I gave her money, would she be more likely to a) use it to feed and educate her children, or b) grunt out nine more children and move to a dislodged glacier floating in the Arctic Ocean?

The interesting part of the conversation came after I politely declined her invitation to fund the nonstop production of doomed babies. She got mad at me. Apparently she analyzed her situation and came to the conclusion that the root cause of her problem was the unwillingness of total strangers in other countries to give her money. And her solution to that problem was to get angry.

You might be wondering, as I was, whether this woman was actually a con artist who wasn't very good at her job, possibly an intern or a trainee. Maybe the experienced con artists in her office were playing a practical joke on her: "Tell him you're stupid and you need money to produce more people like you." I'll never know the real story. But it reminded me of all the times that my point of view differed from other people's.

For example, our current system of world government involves giving the leaders of all the major countries access to buttons that can launch missiles and vaporize unsuspecting citizens. I think a better system would be if every world leader had to walk around with a sack of explosives on his back and every citizen had access to a wristwatch button that would detonate it. My concept has many benefits beyond the obvious entertainment factor and the reduced risk of being vaporized by an incoming missile. For one thing, there would no longer be any such thing as a "slow news day." And the boring pack of lies called the State of the Union speech would last about thirty seconds. I have to think taxes would be abolished altogether. We wouldn't need all the tax money anyway: The military would be unnecessary and the economic stimulus from eliminating taxes would make all the poor people incredibly wealthy, or so I've been told. And if we needed a highway or a dam built, we could give our president a trowel and then place one finger menacingly over the wristwatch button and say, "Start working, Goober." I realize that my concept would degrade the prestige of the presidency, but I don't think that prestige was doing me any good anyway.

Speaking of world leaders, there's still time to join Dogbert's New Ruling Class (DNRC) and rule by his side when he conquers the planet and makes everyone else our domestic servants. To become a member of the DNRC, just sign up for the free *Dilbert* newsletter that is distributed whenever I feel like it, usually four times a year.

To subscribe or unsubscribe, go to www.dilbert.com. If you have problems with the automated subscription method, write to newsletter@unitedmedia.com.

S.Adams

Scott Adams

Panel 1: YOUR NEW CEO IS THE MOST POWERFUL WOMAN IN THE HI-TECH INDUSTRY.

Panel 2: I RECOMMEND EXPLOITING HER FAME IN YOUR ADVERTISEMENTS.

Panel 3: WHY DO I HAVE TO BE THE ONE TO SUGGEST IT?

CEOs LOVE THIS SORT OF THING.

Panel 4: MY CONSULTANT THINKS YOU SHOULD BE FEATURED IN OUR AD CAMPAIGN.

Panel 5: IS THAT BECAUSE I'M YOUR NEW CEO AND THE MOST POWERFUL WOMAN IN OUR INDUSTRY?

Panel 6: UM... YES, THAT'S WHY.

REMEMBER TO ASK ABOUT TAN LINES.

CEO AS SPOKESPERSON

SHOULDN'T I HOLD UP OUR PRODUCT INSTEAD OF LEANING ON A CHAIR?

NO!

THAT HELPED YOUR HAIR BUT YOU'RE STILL DRESSED LIKE A NUN.

20

21

28

29

32

44

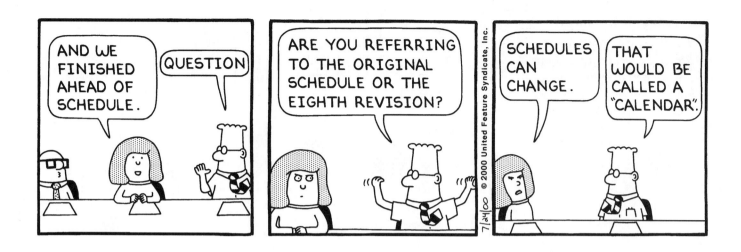

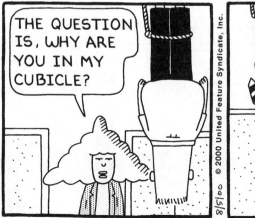

51

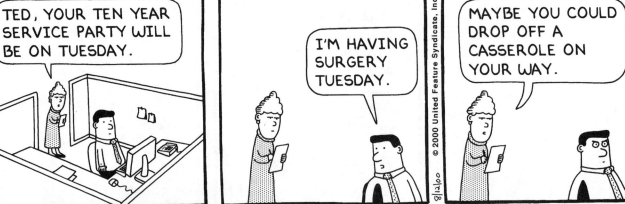

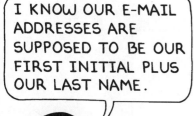

56

66

67

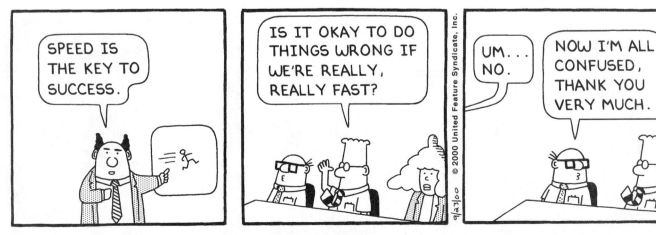

71

THE EVIL H.R. DIRECTOR

WHAT NEW EVIL DO YOU BRING ME, UNION STEWARD STUART?

EMPLOYEES SHOULD NOT BE ALLOWED TO MOVE COMPANY COMPUTERS. THAT'S UNION WORK.

THAT'S OLD EVIL.

IT'S NEW IF WE INCLUDE PDAS AND LAPTOPS.

I LIKE THE CUT OF YOUR GIBLETS.

OUR NEW OFFICE BUILDING WILL BE AN ARCHITECTURAL MASTERPIECE!

THE VOICES IN MY HEAD ARE SHOUTING "NO STORAGE SPACE! NO STORAGE SPACE!"

WHAT IS HAPPENING TO ME?

IT'S CALLED EXPERIENCE.

DOGBERT CONSULTS

YOU NEED TO REORGANIZE BY CUSTOMER TYPE.

ONE DIVISION WOULD FOCUS ON SELLING TO FEEBLE-MINDED PEOPLE.

ARE YOU GESTURING AT ME BECAUSE I WOULD WORK IN THAT DIVISION?

WHAT'S YOUR SECOND GUESS?

89

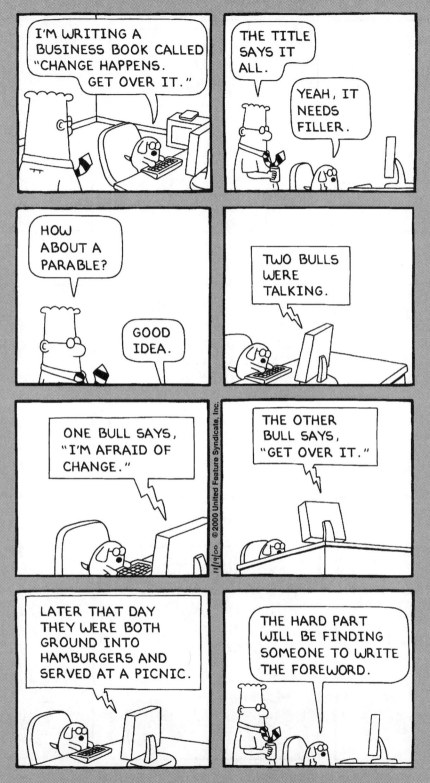

98

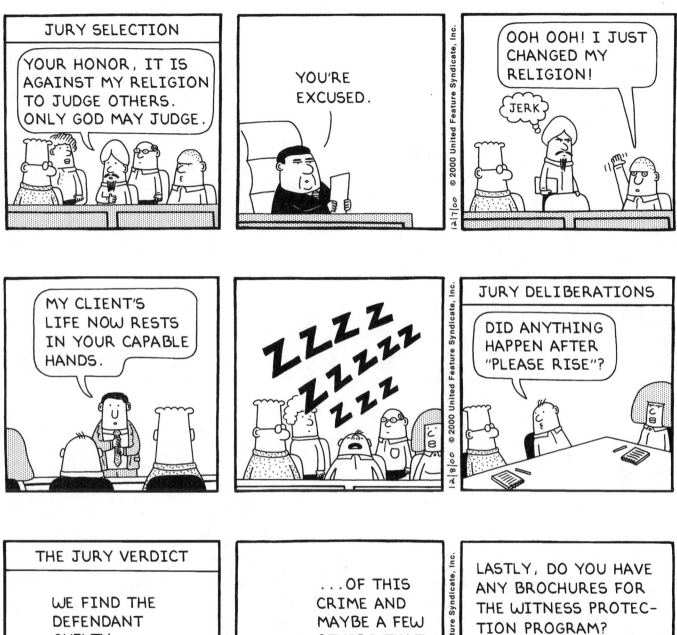

JURY SELECTION

YOUR HONOR, IT IS AGAINST MY RELIGION TO JUDGE OTHERS. ONLY GOD MAY JUDGE.

YOU'RE EXCUSED.

OOH OOH! I JUST CHANGED MY RELIGION!

JERK

MY CLIENT'S LIFE NOW RESTS IN YOUR CAPABLE HANDS.

ZZZZ ZZZZ ZZZ ZZ

JURY DELIBERATIONS

DID ANYTHING HAPPEN AFTER "PLEASE RISE"?

THE JURY VERDICT

WE FIND THE DEFENDANT GUILTY...

...OF THIS CRIME AND MAYBE A FEW OTHERS THAT DIDN'T COME UP.

LASTLY, DO YOU HAVE ANY BROCHURES FOR THE WITNESS PROTECTION PROGRAM?

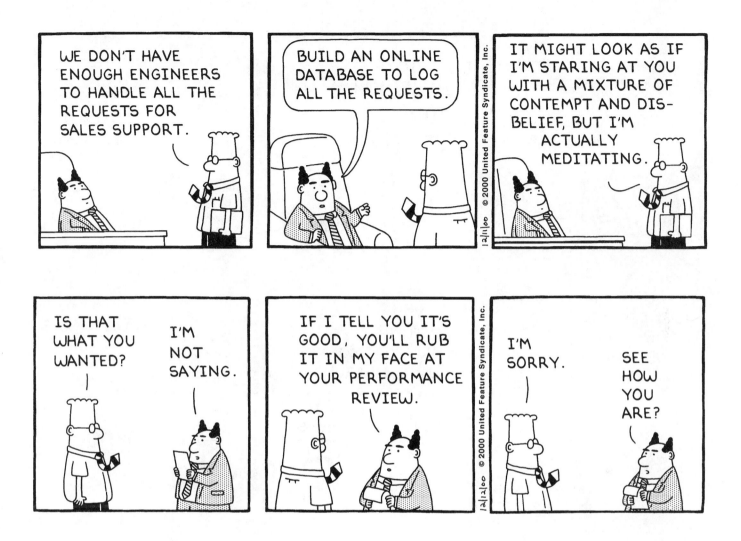

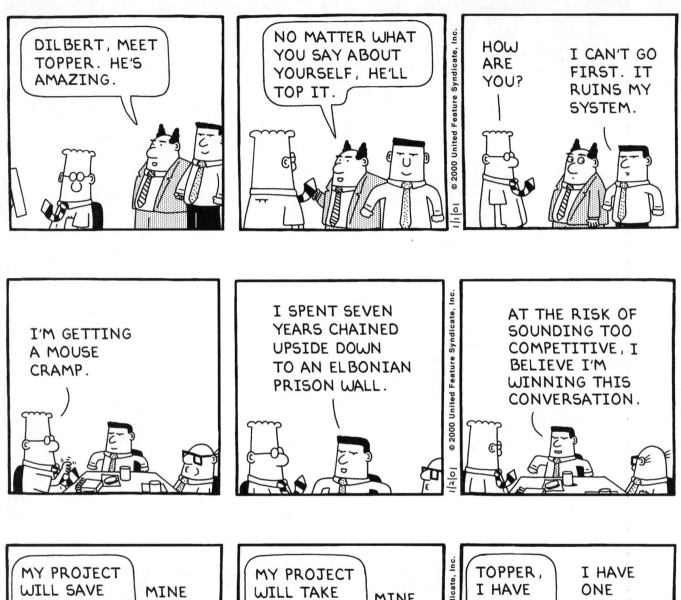

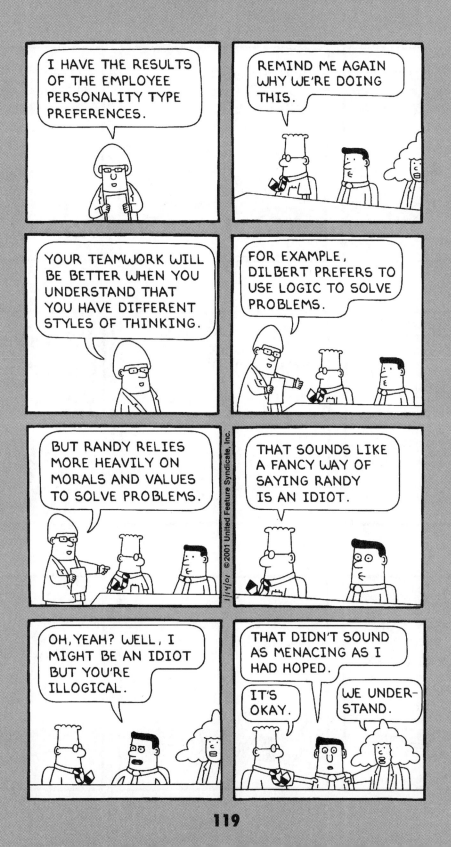